W9-AHB-758

I
LOVE
OUR
WATER

Carol Greene

Enslow Elementary, an imprint of Enslow Publishers, Inc.
Enslow Elementary® is a registered trademark of Enslow Publishers, Inc.

Original edition published as *Caring for Our Water* in 1991.

Library of Congress Cataloging-in-Publication Data

Greene, Carol.
  I love our water / by Carol Greene.
      p. cm. — (I love our Earth)
  Summary: "Find out why water is important, and how people can protect it."—Provided by publisher.
  Includes Index.
  ISBN 978-0-7660-4042-7
  1. Water—Pollution—Juvenile literature. 2. Water—Juvenile literature. 3. Environmental protection—Juvenile literature. I. Title.
  TD422.G74 2012
  628.1'68—dc23   2011023715

Future editions:
Paperback ISBN 978-1-4644-0138-1
ePUB ISBN 978-1-4645-1045-8
PDF ISBN 978-1-4646-1045-5

Printed in the United States of America

042012 Lake Book Manufacturing, Inc., Melrose Park, IL

10 9 8 7 6 5 4 3 2 1

To Our Readers: We have done our best to make sure all Internet Addresses in this book were active and appropriate when we went to press. However, the author and the publisher have no control over and assume no liability for the material available on those Internet sites or on other Web sites they may link to. Any comments or suggestions can be sent by e-mail to comments@enslow.com or to the address on the back cover.

♻ Enslow Publishers, Inc., is committed to printing our books on recycled paper. The paper in every book contains 10% to 30% post-consumer waste (PCW). The cover board on the outside of each book contains 100% PCW. Our goal is to do our part to help young people and the environment too!

Photo Credits: © 2011 Photos.com, a division of Getty Images. All rights reserved., pp. 1, 8, 13, 16, 19; AP Images, p. 15; Shutterstock.com pp. 3, 4–5, 7, 11, 20, 21.

Cover Photo: © 2011 Photos.com, a division of Getty Images. All rights reserved.

Enslow Elementary
an imprint of

Enslow Publishers, Inc.
40 Industrial Road
Box 398
Berkeley Heights, NJ 07922
USA
http://www.enslow.com

Contents

About three-quarters of the earth
is covered by water.

What Is It?

The earth is mostly made of it. Your body is mostly made of it. All living things need it to stay alive.

What is it? Water.

Water covers much of the earth. But most of it is in the oceans. It is salt water and you can't drink it.

Water without salt is called fresh water. You can find it in rivers and streams, lakes and ponds.

But most fresh water is frozen into ice in cold parts of the world. So people can use only a small part of all the water in the world. But that small part is enough— if we take good care of it.

This mountain lake contains fresh water.

A truck sprays water on a field of crops.

Why Is Water Important?

All plants, animals, and people need water to live. Without water, they cannot use their food or get rid of wastes. If you went more than a week without water, you would die.

People also use water to grow plants for food. It takes a lot of water to grow a crop of wheat or corn. Much of this water comes from rain. But in dry places, people must bring water to their crops.

Some plants and animals make their home in water. Fish, whales, dolphins, water lilies, and cattails will soon die out of water.

Water also cleans things. People use it to wash dishes and clothes, take showers and baths, brush teeth, flush toilets, and many other things.

Factories use a lot of water. They use it to clean things and to make things. But mostly they use it to cool things, such as steel.

People also use water to make power. Then they use the power to make heat or light or to run machines.

Sometimes people move things on water. Ships carry goods across the ocean. Barges carry goods up and down rivers.

Water is important for all these reasons. But it is also important because it is beautiful—and fun. People can swim in it or sail or ski. They can look at a waterfall or a lake at sunset. Some people write music or poems about it. They show how beautiful water is.

Playing in a pool is always fun.

What Can Happen to Water?

Water can get dirty. This happens when **pollutants** from factories get into it. Pollutants are harmful things left over after burning or making something.

Other factory pollutants can get into the air. There they mix with rain and fall to earth again. This is called **acid rain**. It harms plants and trees. It kills fish and other water animals. It can even harm buildings and bridges.

Water gets dirty from farm wastes, too. Some farmers use too many pest-killers to kill weeds and insects. They use too many fertilizers to make crops grow tall. These things mix with rain or snow. They get into rivers, lakes, and streams and make the water dirty.

Pollutants enter the water and make it unsafe to use.

Water can also get dirty from sewers. Sewer water is full of wastes, garbage, and soap. Sometimes people clean sewer water, so it can be used again. But sometimes they just let it run into rivers, lakes, or oceans.

People also spill things into the water by accident. Ships spilling oil are a big problem right now.

Dirty water spreads diseases. Sometimes people die from drinking it. In some places, people have run out of clean, fresh water.

Dirty water can also kill plants, fish, birds, and other animals. It can make our rivers, lakes, and oceans ugly and smelly.

This pelican is covered in oil that spilled into the sea.

Keeping our water clean is very important.

What Can We Do?

The earth can have clean water if people stop dumping things into it. People can make laws to stop factories from dumping pollutants. Factories can find better ways to get rid of their pollutants.

Farmers can use safe ways to kill pests and make crops grow tall.

People can clean up all the water and wastes that run through sewers.

People can also be more careful. They can build better ships to carry oil. They can try to use less oil, too.

Cleaning up our water and keeping it clean will take hard work. It will cost money.

But the earth must have clean water.

All living things need water
to stay alive.

What Can You Do?

You can help keep water clean, too. Here are some things that you can do.

- Don't throw litter in or around water. (Don't throw litter anywhere except into trash bins.)

- Don't let the water run while you brush your teeth. Just turn it on to wet your brush and to rinse. This will save clean water.

- Don't let the water run to get yourself a cold drink. Keep a bottle in the refrigerator for drinks. You'll save more clean water.

- Take short showers instead of baths. Short showers use less clean water, too.

- Draw a picture or write a poem about water. Show what you have done to your family and friends.

Turn off the water while you brush your teeth.

Words to Know

acid rain—Rain, snow, or sleet with pollutants in it.

fresh water—Water without much salt in it.

ice—Frozen water.

ocean—A large body of salt water.

oil—A greasy liquid that can be burned.

pollutant (poh LOOT ent)—A thing left over after burning or making something. It is harmful to the earth.

salt water—Water with a lot of salt in it.

sewer—A large pipe, most often under the ground, that carries away water and wastes.

water—A liquid that falls from the clouds and covers much of the earth.

Learn More

Books

O'Ryan, Ellie. *Easy to Be Green: Simple Activities You Can Do to Save the Earth*. New York: Simon & Schuster, 2009.

Oxlade, Chris. *Down the Drain: Conserving Water*. Chicago: Heinemann-Raintree, 2005.

Price, Sean. *Water Pollution*. Tarrytown, N.Y.: Marshall Cavendish, 2008.

Strauss, Rochelle. *One Well: The Story of Water on Earth*. Tonawanda, N.Y.: Kids Can Press, 2007.

Web Sites

EPA WaterSense Kids
<http://www.epa.gov/watersense/kids/index.html>

Planet Pals
<http://www.planetpals.com>

Index